S0-AIV-306

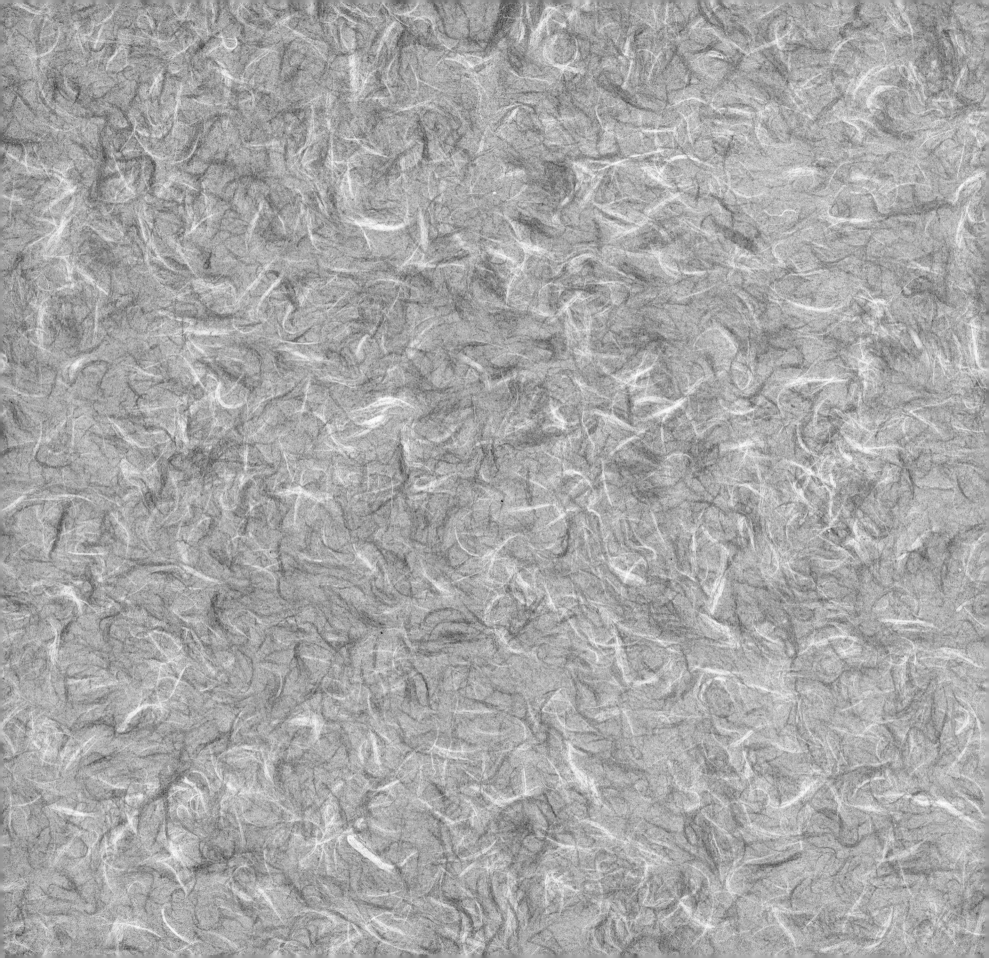

SEASONS

Other books by Warabé Aska

Who Goes to the Park
Who Hides in the Park

PHILIP LARKIN

The Trees

The trees are coming into leaf
Like something almost being said . . .
Last year is dead, they seem to say,
Begin afresh, afresh, afresh.

Philip Larkin (England, 1922–85)

The Trees in High Windows
(Faber & Faber, London, 1974)

SEASONS

WARABÉ ASKA *with poetry selected by Alberto Manguel*

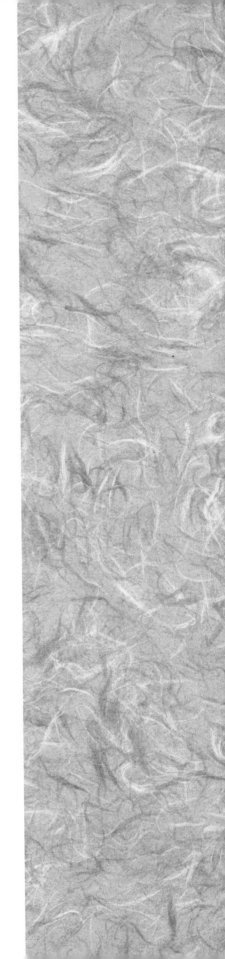

DOUBLEDAY   TORONTO   NEW YORK   LONDON   SYDNEY   AUCKLAND

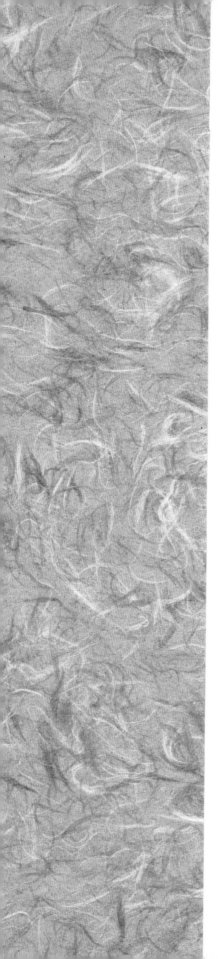

Copyright ©1990 by Warabé Aska (Takeshi Masuda)

All rights reserved. No part of this work may be reproduced or transmitted in any form or by any means, electronic or mechanical, including photocopying and recording, or by any information storage or retrieval system, without permission in writing from the publisher.

CANADIAN CATALOGUING IN PUBLICATION DATA

Aska, Warabé
 Seasons

Poems.
ISBN 0-385-25265-X

1. Seasons in art – Juvenile literature.
2. Seasons – Juvenile poetry. I. Manguel, Alberto, 1948–   . II. Title.

ND249.A84A4 1990   j759.11   C90-093583-9

Library of Congress Cataloging-in-Publication data applied for
ISBN 0-385-25265-X   0-385-41633-4 (lib. bdg.)

Production editor: MAGGIE REEVES
Design by ROSS MAH DESIGN ASSOCIATES
Typesetting by TRIGRAPH INC
Separations by COLOUR TECHNOLOGIES
Printed and bound by NEW INTERLITHO, ITALY

Published in Canada by
DOUBLEDAY CANADA LIMITED
105 Bond Street, Toronto, Ontario   M5B 1Y3

Published simultaneously in the USA by
DOUBLEDAY   A division of Bantam Doubleday Dell Inc.
666 Fifth Avenue, New York, New York   10103

Care has been taken to trace ownership of copyright material in this book and to secure permissions. The publishers will gladly receive any information that will enable them to rectify errors or omissions affecting references or credit lines in subsequent editions.

"The Trees" from High Windows by Philip Larkin. Copyright © 1974 by Philip Larkin. Reprinted by permission of Farrar, Straus & Giroux, Inc., and Faber & Faber Ltd.; "Ring-Around", an anonymous poem, from The Singing Game by Iona and Peter Opie (1985). Reprinted by permission of Oxford University Press. "The Pleasures of Merely Circulating". Copyright 1936 by Wallace Stevens and renewed 1964 by Holly Stevens. Reprinted from The Collected Poems of Wallace Stevens, by permission of Alfred A. Knopf Inc.; Noel Stock: Love Poems Of Ancient Egypt. Copyright © 1962 Noel Stock. Reprinted by permission of New Directions Publishing Corporation; "The Puppeteers" by Fujiwara no Tadamachi from Anthology Of Japanese Literature ed. by Donald Keene. Reprinted by permission of Grove Weidenfield. Copyright © 1955 by Grove Press, Inc.; "The Painted Ceiling" from The Complete Poetical Works Of Amy Lowell by Amy Lowell. Copyright © 1955 by Houghton Mifflin Company. Copyright © 1983 renewed by Houghton Mifflin Co., Brinton P. Roberts, Esquire, and G. D'Andelot Belin, Esquire. Reprinted by permission of Houghton Mifflin Company; "Prayer to the Moon" in The Prayers Of African Religion © 1975 J.S. Mbiti, reproduced by permission of SPCK, London; "Woman Skating" from Margaret Atwood's Selected Poems, selection © Margaret Atwood (Toronto: Oxford University Press Canada, 1976; Boston: Houghton Mifflin Company, 1976); "Snow" in The Pillow Book by Sei Shonagon, translated from the Japanese by Ivor Morris. Reprinted by permission of Oxford University Press.

Introduction

THROUGHOUT EACH of the four seasons, Nature shows us many faces.

By coming into contact with these and feeling the rhythms of their comings and goings, I am always able to make fresh discoveries and find new surprises. This book, *Seasons*, is filled with the sense of wonder which I have gained from communing with Nature.

Wouldn't you like to take each one of these pictures and try to discover something marvellous in them for yourself?

Here are some games I thought up . . .(but I'm sure you and your friends can think of many more). . . .

1 The picture on the cover is really made up of lots of other pictures. In fact, I took one image from every picture in the book and put it into the one on the cover. Can you find *all* of them?

2 One of my pictures, the one on page 19, is a SECRET picture, because inside I decided to hide ten sorts of VERY SECRET ANIMALS. I bet you can't find all of them in less than ten minutes!

If this book helps you to discover the joy and wonder of Nature, that will make me happier than I ever could have hoped.

I dedicate this book to my beloved wife Keiko, to my three children Haydn, Mari and Kohta who soothe my heart, and to my wonderful friends who always give me so much encouragement.

Warabé Aska

ANONYMOUS (ENGLAND)

Ring-Around

Round the green gravel the grass is so green,
And all the fine ladies that ever were seen;
Washed in milk and dressed in silk,
The last shall marry the love of her dream.

Anonymous (England, c. 1900)

"Ring-Around" in The Singing Game *by Iona and Peter Opie (Oxford University Press, 1985). Ring games are some of the oldest games played by people. In England there are many versions of this rhyme, the earliest one from 1835. This version was recorded in the Forest of Dean, and no one knows the names of the children who made it up.*

WALLACE STEVENS

The Garden Flew Round

The garden flew round with the angel,
The angel flew round with the clouds,
And the clouds flew round and the clouds flew round
And the clouds flew round with the clouds.

Wallace Stevens (USA, 1879–1955)

From "The Pleasures of Merely Circulating" in Collected Poems *(Alfred Knopf, 1972).*
After working as a reporter and an independent lawyer, Stevens took a legal job at the age of forty in an insurance company. He remained there until his death, and for the longest time, his colleagues had no idea that at the desk next to theirs sat one of the great geniuses of modern poetry.

 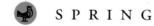

FEDERICO GARCÍA LORCA

Meditation in the Rain

Oh, the quiet of the rain in the garden!
My heart suffers change in this chaste landscape,
In a rumour of thoughts so sad and humble
It settles deep down inside me a rustle of doves.

Federico García Lorca (Spain,
1898–1936)

"Meditation in the Rain" from
"Meditacion bajo la lluvia" in
Libro de Poemas 1918–1920
(Alianza Editorial, Madrid,
1984). Translated from the
Spanish by Alberto Manguel.
Lorca believed that a poet was
someone gifted with something he
called duende, which in Spanish
means "imp". Lorca's "imp" led
him to write verse inspired by
Spain's Arab and gypsy roots, and
powerful poetic plays. Lorca was
murdered by Nationalist soldiers
during the Spanish Civil War.

W. H. DAVIES

The Rainbow

It was the rainbow that gave you birth
And left thee all her lovely hues.

W.H. Davies (Wales, 1871–1940)

"The Rainbow" from "The Kingfisher" in Complete Poems *(Faber & Faber, 1963).*
As a young man, Davies traveled throughout North America on foot and ended up looking for gold in the Klondike. He loved nature and the outdoors life, and tells of his adventures in The Autobiography of a Super-Tramp, *published in 1908.*

Song of the Soul

Oh night that was my guide!
Oh darkness dearer than the morning's pride,
Oh night that joined the lover
To the beloved bride
Transfiguring them each into the other.

St John of the Cross
(Spain, 1542–91)

"Song of the Soul" from "Cántico
espiritual" in Poems *(Collins,*
London, 1951). Translated from
the Spanish by Roy Campbell.
A contemporary of Cervantes and
of Shakespeare, St John of the
Cross was the finest mystical poet
of Spain's Golden Age. He wrote
very little, less than 1,000 lines
altogether, but the beauty of his
language remains unsurpassed.

EMILY DICKINSON

Sun

I'd rather recollect a setting
Than own a rising sun
Though one is beautiful forgetting —
And true the other one.

Emily Dickinson (USA, 1830–86)

"Sun" in Complete Poems,
*edited by Thomas H. Johnson
(Faber & Faber, 1970).
Brought up in a strict Calvinist
home, Dickinson led a quiet,
withdrawn life during which she
wrote over 1,700 poems. Only
seven of her poems were published
during her lifetime, and her first
book did not appear until four
years after her death.*

ANONYMOUS (GERMANY)

Summer Song

Summer's here — joy draws near.
Meadows flower — colours shower.
Sun rekindles — sorrow dwindles.

Anonymous (Germany, 13th century)

This song is one of a collection of lyrics written in Latin and discovered in an abbey in Bavaria (because of this they were called "Carmina Burana" or "Bavarian Songs"). The collection includes love poems, satires and comic verse, and was set to music by the composer Carl Orff.

Flowers

Blossoms crowd the branches: too beautiful to endure.
Thinking of you, I break into bloom again.

Hsueh T'ao (China, 768–831)

"Flowers" from "Spring-Gazing Song" in A Book of Women Poets *(Schocken Books, New York, 1980). Translated from the Chinese by Carolyn Kizer. Hsueh T'ao was the daughter of a government official and at the age of ten became a "singing girl" at the imperial court. Only ninety poems of her entire output have survived.*

Love Song

I am first among your loves,
like a freshly sprinkled garden of grass
and perfumed flowers.
Your voice gives life, like nectar.
To see you is more than food or drink.

Anonymous (Egypt, c. 1500 BC)

"Love Song" in Love Poems of Ancient Egypt *(New Directions, 1962). Translated from the Ancient Egyptian by Ezra Pound and Noel Stock.*

The Puppeteers

Ceaseless wanderers from of old, the puppeteers,
Over all the earth searching ever a new home.
They pitch their tents and sing
in the night to the mountain moon.

Fujiwara no Tadamachi (Japan, 1097–1164)

"The Puppeteers" from Anthology of Japanese Literature *edited by Donald Keene (Grove Press, 1955). Translated by Burton Watson. Throughout the 11th and 12th centuries, there were groups of gypsy-like people who wandered throughout Japan performing puppet shows and magic tricks. The poet Fujiwara no Tadamachi wrote this poem in Chinese, considered the "cultured" language of the time.*

Autumn Day

Lord: it is time. The huge summer has gone by.
Now overlap the sundials with your shadows,
and on the meadows let the wind go free.

Command the fruits to swell on the tree and vine;
grant them a few more warm transparent days,
urge them on to fulfillment then, and press
the final sweetness into the heavy wine.

Rainer Maria Rilke (Austria, 1875–1926)

"Autumn Day" in The Selected
Poetry *(Vintage, New York,
1982). Translated from the
German by Stephen Mitchell.
He was a European, born in
Prague of a German-speaking
family, when it came under
Austrian domination, and lived
in Russia, France, and Italy. He
believed that behind everyday
things was a greater reality and he
tried to describe it in his poems.*

ALFONSINA STORNI

Wind

The star, like a cat, turns in the windy sky.
You! fly, if you can, among the autumn trees!

Alfonsina Storni (Argentina, 1892–1938)

"Windy Sky" from "My Sister" in Poemas *(Centro Editor de America Latina, Buenos Aires, 1968). Translated from the Spanish by Alberto Manguel. Storni published her first book,* The Restlessness of the Rosetree *at the age of twenty-four. In this, as in all her books, she tried to escape the male romantic view of what a woman was supposed to be and feel, and in doing so produced poems of great strength and beauty.*

Hurrahing in Harvest

Summer ends now; now, barbarous in beauty, the stooks arise
Around; up above, what wind-walks! what lovely behaviour
Of silk-sack clouds!

*Gerard Manley Hopkins
(England, 1844–89)*

"Hurrahing in Harvest" in Poems
and Prose *(Penguin, 1953).
When he was twenty-four years
old, he became a Jesuit priest. In
his poems, in praise of God and
nature, he invented wonderful
new rhythms and rhymes.
Hopkins published no books
during his lifetime; after his
death, his poems were brought out
by his friend Robert Bridges.*

AMY LOWELL

Adventures

It's a little bit sad, when you seem very near
    To adventures and things of that sort,
Which nearly begin, and then don't; and you know
    It is only because you are short.

Amy Lowell (USA, 1874–1925)

"Adventure" from "The Painted Ceiling" in The Poems of Amy Lowell (Houghton Mifflin, 1955). Lowell was an intelligent and original poet, a fierce defender of modern poetry, and a staunch believer in women's rights.

ANONYMOUS (ETHIOPIA)

Prayer to the Moon

May you be for us a moon of joy and happiness.

Let the stranger come to the end of his journey.

And those who remain home dwell safely in their houses . . . .

May you be a moon of harvest and of calves.

May you be a moon of restoration and good health.

Anonymous (Ethiopia)

"Prayer to the Moon" in Prayers of African Religion *edited by Professor John Mbiti (The Society for Promoting Christian Knowledge, London, 1972). Translated from the Amharic by Professor John Mbiti.*
This prayer is chanted with the rise of the new moon. There are similar Ethiopian prayers, thanking the sun for rising and the rain for falling.

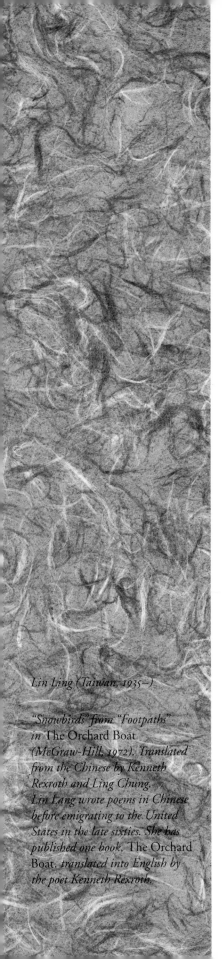

LIN LING

Snowbirds

A pure white feather floats down.
Oh, at that moment
We both hope that happiness
May also be like a white bird,
Quietly descending.

Lin Ling (Taiwan, 1935–)

*"Snowbirds" from "Footpaths"
in* The Orchard Boat
*(McGraw-Hill, 1972). Translated
from the Chinese by Kenneth
Rexroth and Ling Chung.
Lin Ling wrote poems in Chinese
before emigrating to the United
States in the late sixties. She has
published one book,* The Orchard
Boat, *translated into English by
the poet Kenneth Rexroth.*

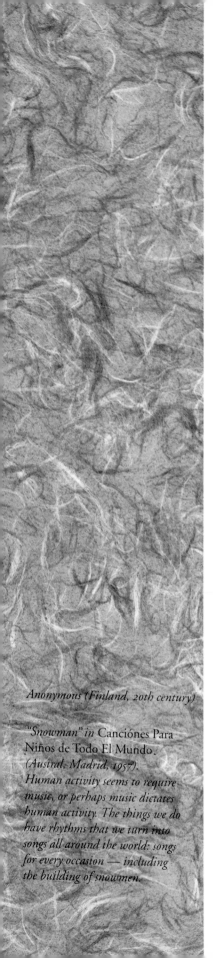

Snowman

The snowman in the snow —
How do you know
That *he* hasn't made *you* instead?

Anonymous (Finland, 20th century)

"Snowman" in Canciónes Para
Niños de Todo El Mundo.
(Austral, Madrid, 1957).
Human activity seems to require
music, or perhaps music dictates
human activity. The things we do
have rhythms that we turn into
songs all around the world: songs
for every occasion — including
the building of snowmen.

MARGARET ATWOOD

Woman Skating

With arms wide the skater
turns, leaving her breath like a diver's
trail of bubbles.

Seeing the ice
as what it is, water.

Margaret Atwood (Canada, 1939–)

"Woman Skating" from "Woman Skating" in Procedures for Underground *(Oxford University Press, Toronto, 1976). Atwood, now celebrated as a fiction writer, began her literary career as a poet. Her first book won the Canadian Governor General's Award in 1966, when she was twenty-seven years old.*

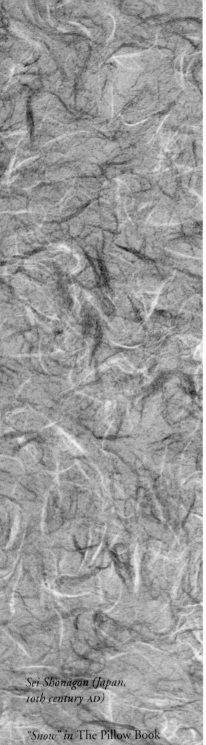

SEI SHONĀGON

Snow

As though pretending to be blooms
The snowflakes scatter in the winter sky.

*Sei Shonāgon (Japan,
10th century AD)*

"Snow" in The Pillow Book
*(Penguin, 1971). Translated from
the Japanese by Ivor Morris.
Sei Shonāgon was a lady-in-wait-
ing at the Court of the Japanese
Empress one thousand years ago.
The Pillow Book is a wonderful
record of things she liked and dis-
liked, minute observations, lists
and poems.*

VICTOR HUGO

Dreams

Sometimes, out in the shapeless space,
Look there, my child! And you shall see!
A sudden planet passes by —
It flies, approaches, runs, draws nigh.

Of such fantastic spheres the universe is made.

Victor Hugo (France, 1802–85)

"Dreams" from "The Struggles and the Dreams." Translated from the French by Alberto Manguel. Hugo was the author of great romantic novels such as Les Misérables and The Hunchback of Notre Dame. He was also a powerful poet and an eloquent defender of civil liberties.

Hidden Animals

1. Giraffes
2. Horses
3. Peacocks
4. Elephant
5. Ostrich
6. Rabbits
7. Sheep
8. Deer
9. Owl
10. Lion

List of Paintings

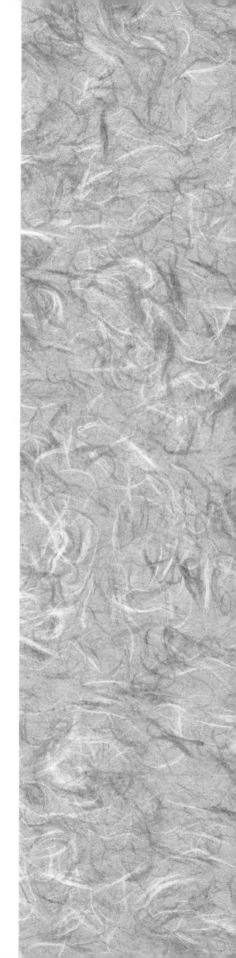

Acknowledgements

I would like to thank Alberto Manguel for selecting the delightful poems from the marvellous array of poetry in the world, and also thank the publishers and copyright holders for permission to use them. My thanks to the collectors of the paintings for allowing their inclusion in this book.

I am grateful to Robin Muller and to Margaret Thomson Nightingale who gave me the great opportunity of meeting John Pearce, who proposed this book.

Warabé Aska